INVASION OF GOD'S GLORY

VOL. 2

Now that we have come out, it's time to go in

ELDER VALERIE BOONE

WESTBOW®
PRESS
A DIVISION OF THOMAS NELSON
& ZONDERVAN

WestBow Press books may be ordered through booksellers or by contacting:

WestBow Press
A Division of Thomas Nelson & Zondervan
1663 Liberty Drive
Bloomington, IN 47403
www.westbowpress.com
1 (866) 928-1240

ISBN: 978-1-4908-6961-2 (sc)

Library of Congress Control Number: 2015902278

Print information available on the last page.

WestBow Press rev. date: 3/16/2015

CONTENTS

DEDICATION

This book is dedicated to the memory and in the honor of my son
Qonta Charlie Waddell and all of the families in Baltimore City
who have been believing for an invasion of God's Glory in this city.

CHAPTER 1

THE KNOCK ON THE DOOR

On April 21st, 2009, at 5:30 am. in the morning, there was a knock on my apartment door. I said, 'Who is it?' My son said, 'It's me, mom, Qonta.' Before I opened the door, I knew that it was my son because every mother knows their child's voice beyond any other voice. So I opened the door and at the door was Qonta my son and two other young men that were standing close to him.

Then Qonta began to talk to me. He said, 'Mom, don't look at their faces. Don't say anything,' then he put his finger on my lips.

That's when I said, 'What do you mean? I *will* look! I *will* speak! This is *my* house!' Then I began to look at them and at that time, my eyes saw the guns that they had in their hands, but I kept on talking to them. I remember saying to them, 'You all have got yourself caught up in the things of this world. You are running around in the middle of the night doing things that you know is wrong. Did your parents raise you like that? No, but because you came to the right door this morning. I will be praying for each one of you.'

They did not respond or talk directly to me. Their attention was on my son. They told him to sit down on the kitchen chair and they gave him

1

a cell phone to dial a phone number and tell the person on the other end of the line to bring the money. My son did what they had said, but the person never pick up the phone.

One of the young men that was pointing the gun at my son the whole time he kept turning the gun sideways. I could see everything with my natural eye but my mind was in the spiritual realm.

Galatians 5:25 (NIV)

'Since we are living by the Spirit, let us follow the Spirit leading in every part of our lives.' (NLT)

After the call was made, the other young man stayed closer to the door looking out with the apartment door halfway open. I knew then there was someone else outside in the parking lot.

When you set the atmosphere of God in your home, evil cannot overtake it. Not ever. Also your lifestyle must line up with kingdom living.

Exodus 24:17 (NLT)

Now the appearance of the glory of the Lord was like a devouring fire on the top of the mountain in the sight of the people of Israel. (NKJV)

Isaiah 60:1

Arise, shine for your light has come and the glory of the Lord has risen upon you. (NKJV)

Then my son Qonta said he had to go to the bathroom, the young man who told him to make the call said no. Both of the young men had a gun in their hands.

So Qonta got up and began to fight with one of the young men. They went toward the hall and my bedroom while the other young man stayed at the door.

That's when I began to pray in the Spirit, but my tongues was so different this time. I always pray in tongues, but this time I began to prophesied first to the young man at the door. His eyes looked as if every word I said that he had heard it before. I remember talking about his grandmother and mother praying for him . Now remember, I have never seen these young men before in my life. He began to respond by saying 'Yes ma'am' over and over and by that time, another young man came in the front door. When he stepped in the door, I looked at him and I was still speaking in tongues. He lifted up both of his hands in the air, went in the room where my son and the other young man were fighting and began to help pull my son out of the apartment door. My son was fighting for his life.

See, you must understand. When we raise and pray for our children, it is multi-generational because the Kingdom is more than us. I have and always will teach my children and my spiritual children that the wages of sin is death, but the gift of God is eternal life in Christ.

Cross References: Genesis 2:17 (NKJ)

But you must not eat from the tree of the knowledge of good and evil for when you eat from it, you will certainly die. (NIV)

Genesis 2:17 does not say that you will go to Hell. It says you will 'certainly die.' We must teach our children the Word. We must relay our children foundation again. It's time to lay down your religion and teach the next generation about having an intimate relationship with Jesus and God.

As I said first I was in the living room area of my apartment. I don't know how I got in the kitchen area. The Spirit lifted me up. The angel of the Lord is always with me. His name is the captain of the host Jesus, my King, my Protector, my Lord!

The last young man went out the door and looked around as if he had seen a ghost. His eyes said, 'What is this presence in this house?' He closed the door behind himself. That was the last time that I saw my 24 year old son alive on this earth.

Qonta Charlie Waddell's body was found at 10:00 am. on April 21, 2009. He was shot four times to the head and thrown into an alley.

You may ask, 'Why did they kill Elder Boone's son?' It is because my son chose the lifestyle of a drug dealer. I love my son no matter what . He is still my son, but my part was to live a lifestyle before him and be a watchmen over his soul. That's what this book is about. Sacrifice.

The word 'sacrifice' means 'the act of giving up. Something that you want to keep especially in order to get or do something else or to help someone else.'

Qonta died six days after his birthday. The number six means the number of man. God is always at work in everything in your life. For the Boone family, Qonta's life was a gift from God and we thank God for the 24 years of life that he had on this earth. But now Qonta is in a higher level of consciousness in God. He is now all spirit and when I look at his son Tai'Juane who is now twelve years old, we can see Qonta's spirit in him. The number 12 is God's government.

If Jesus paid it all, why then must I become the next sacrifice? Qonta's life is not for sin. That's all paid in full by Jesus. This one is for life and for the Kingdom's purpose. This is the sacrifice made upon entering into the Kingdom work that we are called to do in the earth for God-Covenant Community. Every house must have a sacrifice.

Isaiah 41:4

Who has done such mighty deeds summoning each new generation from the beginning of time it is I the Lord the First and the Last. I alone am He. (NLT)

Hebrews 10:10

It is through that divine will that we have been set free from sin through the offering of Jesus Christ as our sacrifice once for all. (WNT)

CHAPTER 2

THE FUNERAL

Qonta C. Waddell was born on April 15, 1985. His sunset was April 21, 2009 and his funeral was on Saturday, April 25, 2009. Qonta entered this life a double blessing because he was the surviving twin. Qonta received his primary education at Greater Grace Christian Academy where he was known as the great debater because of his ability to make a point. He never gave up on an argument. Qonta gave me my first grandson. Qonta gave me courage and boldness that I have never had before. I am grateful and honored to be his mother. I carried him and his brother for nine months in my belly.

Genesis 25:23 (NKJ)

The Lord said to her, 'Two nations are in your womb and two peoples from within you will be separated. One people will be stronger than the other and the older will serve the younger.

At my son's funeral, all I could do is worship God thanking Him for all He had done for me and my family.

Proverbs 22:6 (NKJ)

Train up a child in the way he should go even when he is old he will not depart from it.

Romans 12:2 (NKJ)

Do not conform to the pattern of this world, but be transformed by the renewing of your mind. Then you will be able to test and approve what God's will is. His good pleasing and perfect will.

This young girl as soon as I laid my eyes on her, I loved her like my daughter. Mika. Qonta came in the house with her. She was only 11 years old. Qonta was 17 going on 18 years old at the time. He said, 'Mom, meet my wife. Her name is Mika. She reminds me of you, Mom. I am going to marry her.'

I said to Qonta, 'She is too young right now son for you.' Qonta looked at me and smiled and said, 'She is going to be my wife.'

This is what Mika wrote in the obituary:

<u>My Message to You</u>

We met when I was 11. Ever since then, I knew I was in Heaven. You were my first love. We shared so many memories together like the time when we went horseback riding and you and the horse fell in the water. We ate big dinners during the holidays and we laughed at the table. You were such a comedian. You thought you were a star in everyone's eyes. I'm lost without you. It's so hard to say goodbye. I know that sometime I will have to move on, but how can I when my best friend is gone? Why did you have to leave me Lil Guy? I didn't get a chance to say goodbye. God will take care of you now. I'll see you when I get on that side of town.

I love you. Mika

This is what my sister wrote:

My Nephew

Qonta, my nephew, little brother and close friend. Words can hardly explain how I feel right now from the time you were in your mother's womb. I know we would have a special connection. I can remember praying that we would have the same birthday. But six days later was good enough! You and I are inseparable because I will see you again. Qonta, you were too fast for this world so God took you home. His time is enough for you.

I love you----you are my heart. Tish

Matthew 20:16 (NIV)

So the last shall be first and the first will be last.

Qonta Family 2008
Mika and TaiJuane

CHAPTER 3

THE TRIAL

Baltimore City Court System cases are so backed up that we did not go to court for Qonta's murder case until three years later. The trial lasted about thirty days. The holy spirit told me when to go to the court house. The first day God sent me into the trail, I walked into courtroom, God shown me how he played his part in each person who entered the courtroom.

The state attorney said there were ten young men who were a part of the plot against my son but only six were brought to trial. They were part of one of the gangs in Baltimore City.

My son was not a part of a gang, but he sold drugs to them. As I sat and listened to the trial, you might think it was about Qonta and his money. But it was personal. When people plot and plan to do something against you, it's always personal jealousy. What does God say about jealousy?

Definition of jealous-feeling ill will and envy; an act or remark.

James 3:14 (NIV)

But if you have bitter jealousy and selfish ambition in your hearts, do not boast and be false to the truth. This is not the wisdom that comes down from above but is earthly, unspiritual demonic.

Genesis 4:8 (NIV)

Cain spoke to Abel his brother and when they were in the field, Cain rose up against his brother Abel and killed him.

James 3:16 (NIV)

For where jealousy and selfish ambition exists, there will be disorder and every vile practice.

This experience for me was wrapped around a big part of my purpose and what I was called to do in the Kingdom of God. When I looked at all the young men sitting on the side of the courtroom and all were black men, it was clear to me that this was a big part of my calling.

The resource center that God was telling me to open up was about men finding out what their purpose and destiny are. They were about 20-35 years old. They looked so lost in their faces. The young men who are in gangs are looking for people who are living a kingdom lifestyle.

Like I said in the first chapter, this experience took my family and I over into a new glory called Chayil for the work of purpose for the Kingdom of God, we became an army 'Chayil Glory.'

Yes, we are the Bride made ready, but we must go over. It's very important that the church understands the difference. We will not lose any more sons to the streets. We are a Chayil Army.

At the end of the trial, one of the young men was completely released. He looked like he was about twenty years old because there was no evidence placing him in the area at the time of killing. But the other young men received life and sixty-five years.

But when it was my turn to speak to the young men, God had already written it in my heart. I said, 'I am more than just Qonta's mother today. I stand as the mouthpiece of God. First of all, you have been forgiven for what you have done. You have been looking for love for all of your young lives. But today you have seen what love looks and sounds like. All you have to do is receive it. Now walk in the newness of God. It's really simple and it's been made clear just for you on this day.

Every one of the gang members began to hold their heads down to the floor. When God steps into the room, all flesh must bow down.

Romans 14:1 (NIV)

Every knee shall bow and every tongue confess.

A word for Baltimore City:

LOVE HAS COME FOR US ALL

CHAPTER 4

IMAGE OF GOD

All my life as long as I could remember I have always loved being close to the men in my life. It started with my two brothers Dwayne and Adrian. My mother was a full-time worker and a single parent. You know how people say they had a praying grandmother? Well, I have a praying mother and she has always prayed for me and my brothers.

But years before, we lived with my grandparents and I lived in a house full of my mother's brothers (my uncles). So I grew up always around men so I have great respect for men and I learned how to be a lady because they always were gentlemen when it came down to dealing with the females in there lives.

Let's see what God says about men:

Genesis 1:27 (NKJ)

So God created man in his own image of God he created him male and female he created them.

I Corinthians 16:13-14 (NKJ)

Be on your guard stand firm in the faith be men of courage be strong do everything in love.

According to these verses, a true man is vigilant against danger, faithful to the truth, brave in the face of opposition, persistent through trials and above all, loving.

I Corinthians 13:11 (NIV)

A true man is someone who has put away childish things. A true man knows what is right and stands firm in the right. A true man is a Godly man. He loves the Lord, he loves life and he loves those whom the Lord has entrusted to his care for.

As women, we must be careful not to take on the mindset of this world because in this day and time women of the world's mindset believe men are something just to make them feel good and feel better about themselves. Some women, not all, have lost the foundation of respect and honor for men.

Some women may have not had a male or father figure in their life. I believe every young girl needs a father figure in their life to help her learn what she needs to know about how to relate to men and what men expect and how they think.

Let's look at the nature of men:

Man as Trinity=spirit, soul and body

Many think that man is a physical being only, there is great danger of any man thinking of himself being only physical.

Let's take a look inside of man:

Sexuality-the feelings behaviors and identities associated with sex.

Sensuality-The quality or state of being sensual or lascivious; excessive devotion to sensual pleasure.

Sociality-The tendency of groups and persons to develop social links and live in communities.

Spirituality-The state or quality of being dedicated to God or religion or spiritual things or values.

1st purpose for God's glory. Man should ponder on and learn to re-examine his life. In the process, he should begin with the primary reason why God created him. For sure, man was not created only to eat, drink and be merry. Man was created and chosen by God for Himself. To serve the Lord God with gladness is to fulfill the very purpose of man's existence.

Psalm 100:2-3 (NKJ)

Serve the Lord with gladness. Come before his presence with singing. Know that the Lord He is God. It is He who has made us and not we ourselves. We are his people and the sheep of his pasture.

Spirit-Formed

Spirit-The word spirit is often used to refer to the consciousness or personality.

Spirit-A manifestation of the spirit of a living person.

Spirit-Comes from the Latin world meaning 'breath.'

Formed-The shape and structure of an object. The body or outward appearance of a person or an animal.

Formed-Manifestation the particular way that something is or appears to be color, texture or composition.

When you come into a mature place in God, you take on his form.

Spirit-Formed-mean living and walking in the image and likeness of God. John 1:14 (NIV)

That when you can see and touch the nature of God character in your life. We are life-giving spirits.

Jesus said to Mary Magdalene, 'Don't touch me.' In Greek, it means 'may, mou, aptou'. It means 'stop clinging to me.' Christ was not telling Mary to not touch Him. She and the other women were already touching Him. He was telling her to stop clinging to Him because He wasn't going to be around for long. He would be turning to the Father. This is something that Mary needed to get used to. John 20:17

Spirit-Form is all about descending from one place in God to another. This was now the third time Jesus appeared to His disciples after He was raised from the dead. John 21:14 (NIV)

Transfiguration and descending is all about spirit form. Take a look at Matthew 17:1-13:(NIV)

After six days, Jesus took with him Peter, James and John, the brother of James and led them up a high mountain. There he was transfigured before them. His face shown like the sun and his clothes became as white as the light. Just then, there appeared before them Moses and Elijah talking with Jesus.

Peter said to Jesus, "Lord, it is good for us to be here. If you wish, I will put up three shelters. One for you, one for Moses and one for Elijah." While he was still speaking, a bright cloud covered them and a voice from the cloud said, "This is my Son, whom I love with him I am well pleased. Listen to him."

Calling all men is all about the army of God.

Greetings...Jude 1:1-2 (NKJ)

1. Jude, a slave of Jesus Christ and a brother of James. To those who are the called loved by God the Father and kept by Jesus Christ.
2. May mercy, peace and love be multiplied to you.

12. These are the ones who are like dangerous reefs at your love feasts. They feast with you nurturing only themselves without fear. They are waterless clouds carried along by winds trees in late autumn. Fruitless twice dead pulled out by the roots.

13. Wild waves of the sea foaming up their shameful deeds wandering stars for whom are reserved the blackness of darkness forever.

14. And Enoch in the seventh generation from Adam prophesied about them. Look the Lord comes with thousands of His holy ones to execute judgment on all and to convict them.

15. Look the Lord comes with thousands of His holy ones to execute judgment on all and to convict them of all their ungodly deeds that they have done in an ungodly way and of all the harsh things ungodly sinners have said against Him.

16. These people are discontented grumblers walking according to their desires their mouths utter arrogant words flattering people for their own advantage.

17. But you dear friends remember the words foretold by the apostles of our Lord Jesus Christ.

18. They told you in the end time there will be scoffers walking according to their own ungodly desires.

19. These people create divisions and are merely natural not having the Spirit.

20. But you dear friends building yourselves up in your most holy faith and praying in the Holy Spirit.

21. Keep yourselves in the love of God expecting the mercy of our Lord Jesus Christ for eternal life.

22. Have mercy on some who doubt.

23. Save others by snatching them from the fire on others have mercy in fear hating even the garment defiled by the flesh.

24. Now to Him who is able to protect you from stumbling and to make you stand in the presence of His glory blameless and with great joy.

25. To the only God our Savior through Jesus Christ our Lord be glory, majesty, power and authority before all time now and forever. Amen. Jude 1:12-25 (NKJ)

CHAPTER 5

CALLING

Calling-A strong desire to spend your life doing a certain kind of work that a person does or should be doing.

Calling-A strong inner impulse toward a particular course of action especially when accompanied by conviction or divine influence.

I believe every man know when God is calling him because He knows them and that not only by their name.

When Christ calls a man, he bids him come and die. It's like that of the first disciples who had to leave home and work to follow Him.

Death in Jesus Christ, the death of the old man.

In every man's life, I believe through God's Word that there is an appointed time when God desires to have fellowship with a man. It will be a time when a man is to separate from the known world around him and follow God into a relationship and trust.

That a man may grow into the purpose of all they were made to be since the foundations of this world.

In Genesis 12:1-20, God tells Abram to leave his father's household onto a land that he was to show him. God said that he would make him a great nation and bless him. When Abram heard this, he was living in his father's household at 75 years old. He was married to Sarai and they both were still part of the Chaldean culture in Ur and under Abram's father Terah. Sometimes God's call is hard to understand, but Abram obeyed God.

He didn't fully leave his father's house, his father Terah went along with him and Terah died in Haran. Genesis 11:32 God truly desired Abram to himself even to the point if he had to remove the parental figure to make that point clear. This is the case many of the tribulations we have going on in our lives is because we have not fully obeyed God in an area He desires us to be with Him.

The aftermath testifies of itself. Now Abram was alone with his wife Sarai and they were to embark on the journey that God designated for them. They would eventually bear a child and slowly God was fulfilling his plan that he called Abram to.

The plan itself being fulfilled by Abram and Sarai believing in what God said and trusting Him at his word.

Moses was separated from his home at the hand of a wicked pharaoh designing to kill Hebrew children. We find that the plan of God was that Moses was to lead his own people from Egypt.

Daniel who within the king's palace witnessed the holiness of God before the Chaldean people.

If John would have stayed in the house of his birth becoming a temple priest and worshipping God under the Levitical system, he would have never preached the baptism of repentance and be the water baptizer of the Messiah whom at the water baptism of John fulfilled God's plan and thus declared the beginning of Christ Jesus' ministry in this world.

Matthew 22:14 (Holman Christian Standard Bible)

For many are called, but few are chosen.

It's when you answer the call than you become the chosen ones God don't say, 'Eeny, meeny, miny, moe.'

Eeny meeny miny moe is used to select a person to be it. God don't play children's games such as tag. We must grow up in this hour and day that we are in because the fullness of time has come.

God walked in the cool of the day with Adam. Genesis 3:8. God comes in the cool of the day to communicate with those to whom He has given life to. The cool of the day is the breezy time of day meaning wind. Yet now men are hiding from God in fear. God's presence is also by his walking. God demands holiness and obedience in man's inner parts so that He can commune with him.

Although he has millions upon millions of people, God always has time for you and it is always personal time. It is true that God is holy and just and almighty, but He is also a friendly God and always there for us.

Even the youths shall faint and be weary and the young men shall utterly fall. Isaiah 40:30(NIV)

Because there is a famine in the world, men all over the world they are dry because they must answer their call back to God. The call is greater than your gifts because you have to lay your gifts down at the feet of Jesus and answer to the call. It will cost you everything.

The Life-Giving Spirit - (Holman Christian Standard Bible)

Therefore, no condemnation now exists for those in Christ Jesus, because the spirit's law of life in Christ Jesus has set you free from the law of sin and of death. What the law could not do since it was limited by the flesh by sending his own Son in flesh like ours under sin domain and as a sin offering in order that the law's requirement would be accomplished in us who do not walk according to the spirit. For those whose lives are according to the flesh, think about the things of the flesh, but those whose lives are according to the spirit about the things of the Spirit. For the mindset of the flesh is death, but the mindset of the Spirit is life and peace for the mindset of the flesh is hostile to God because it does not submit itself to God's law for it is unable to do so. Those whose lives are in the flesh are unable to please God. You however are not in the flesh but in the Spirit since the Spirit of God lives in you. But if anyone does not have the Spirit of Christ, he does not belong to Him. Now if Christ is in you, the body is dead because of sin but the Spirit is life because of righteousness. And if the Spirit of him who raised Jesus from the dead lives in you then He who raised Christ from the dead will also bring your mortal bodies to life through His Spirit who lives in you.

The Holy Spirit's Ministries

So then brothers we are not obligated to the flesh to live according to the flesh, for if you live according to the flesh, you are going to die. But if by the Spirit you put to death the deeds of the body you will live. All those led by God's Spirit are God's sons. For you did not receive a spirit of slavery to fall back into fear, but you received the spirit of adoption by whom we cry out, 'Abba Father.' The Spirit Himself testifies together with our spirit that we are God's children and if children are also heirs of God and co-heirs with Christ seeing that we suffer with Him so that we may also be glorified with Him.

From Groans to Glory

For I consider that the sufferings of this present time are not worth comparing with the logy that is going to be revealed to us. For the creation eagerly awaits with anticipation for God's sons to be revealed. For the creation was subjected to futility not willingly but because of Him who subjected it in the hope that the creation itself will also be set free from the bondage of corruption into the glorious freedom of God's children. For we know that the whole creation has been groaning together with labor pains until now. And not only that, but we ourselves who have the Spirit as the first fruits we also groan within ourselves eagerly waiting for adoption the redemption of our bodies. Now in this hope we were saved yet hope that is seen is not hope because who hopes for what he sees? But if we hope for what we do not see, we eagerly wait for it with patience. In the same way the Spirit also joins to help in our weakness, because we do not know what to pray for as we should but the Spirit Himself intercedes for us with unspoken roaning and He who searches the hearts knows the spirit's mindset because He intercedes for the saints according to the will of God. We know that all things work together for the good of those who love God; those who are called according to His purpose. For those He foreknew, He also predestined to be conformed to the image of His Son so that He would be the firstborn among many brothers. And those He predestined, He also called and those He called He also justified and those He justified He also glorified.

The Believer's Triumph Holman Christian Standard Bible

What then are we to say about these things? If God is for us, who is against us? He did not even spare His own Son, but offered Him up for us all. How will He not also with Him grant us everything? Who can bring an accusation against God's elect?

God is the One who justifies. Who is the one who condemns? Christ Jesus is the One who died but even more has been raised. He also is at the right hand of God and intercedes for us. Who can separate us from the love of Christ? Can affliction or anguish or persecution or famine or nakedness or danger or sword? As it is written. Because of you, we are being put to death all day long. We are counted as sheep to be slaughtered. No, in all these things we are more than victorious through Him who loved us. For I am persuaded that neither death nor life nor angels nor rulers nor things present, nor things to come nor powers nor height nor depth, nor any other created thing will have the power to separate us form the love of God that is in Christ Jesus our Lord. –Romans chapter 8 (HCSB)

Knowing the Person of the Holy Spirit

The Holy Spirit is a part of the Holy Trinity with the Father and Son. In the Old Testament, the Hebrew word 'ruwach' pronounced roo-akh was used when talking about the Spirit. This word means wind, even the wind associated with breath in the New Testament. We can think of the Holy Spirit as the 'breath of God.' The Holy Spirit is a person, not a thing. In fact, as we begin to know the person of the Holy Spirit, we will want to have a closer relationship with Him just as we would the Father or Son.

Although the word 'trinity' is not mentioned in the Bible, we know God is three in one. There are three very distinct persons that make up the Godhead.

Baptism of the Holy Spirit

Matthew 3:11 (HCSB)

I indeed baptize you with water unto repentance, but he who is coming after me mightier than I whose sandals I am not worthy to carry. He will baptize you with the Holy Spirit and fire.

The people of that day had no idea what it meant to be baptized by the Holy Spirit. They may have had ideas, but nobody knew exactly what John meant. Jesus did not speak about the baptism of the Holy Spirit until he prepared to ascend into heaven. Jesus talked to his disciples just before his arrest. He promised to send the Holy Spirit after he departed. He said, "I will pray the Father and he will give you another Helper that he may abide with you forever-the spirit of truth-whom the world cannot receive because it neither sees Him nor knows Him but you know Him for He dwells with you and will be in you. –John 14:16-17

Fire burns away that which is trash, that which is unclean fire purifies and we need the fire of the Holy Spirit to burn away impurity in our soul and we need the warmth of the Holy Spirit to encourage us. He is called the Comforter. He comforts by warming our hearts.

At Pentecost, the Holy Spirit was given to the church. There is no mention of the baptism of the Spirit. The Bible says they were all filled with the Spirit and they were all filled with the Holy Spirit and began to speak with other tongues as the Spirit gave them utterance. Acts 2:4 (HCSB)

Why doesn't it say, 'and they were all baptized with the Holy Spirit?' Isn't that's what Jesus promised would happen? Isn't that's what John said? Isn't that's what the Father promised?

And that's what happened. They were baptized, filled with rivers of living water. John 7:38-39 and given power. There is no distinction. It's all the same. The Holy Spirit has been poured into the hearts of the believers.

CHAPTER 6

GODLY MEN

So the governors and satraps sought to find some charge against Daniel concerning the kingdom but they could find no charge or fault because he was faithful nor was there any error or fault found in him. Then these men said, 'We shall not find any charge against this Daniel unless we find it against him concerning the law of his God

Because Daniel had an excellent spirit and the king gave thought to setting him over the whole realm. The governors and satraps were jealous of Daniel because of God's favor. They looked for ways to discredit him before the king and he could not find no charge or fault because he was faithful to God. Daniel was a statesman; he was in politics. Daniel was thrown into the lion's den. Daniel interpreted dreams. He never changed the interpretations to save himself. Daniel refused to pray to an idol knowing he could be cast into the lion's den. And God delivered Daniel from the lion's den.

In a day when we have a desperate need for godly people in our homes, at work, among friends and as leaders in our cities, perhaps it would do us well to determine the characteristics of a Godly man.

A Godly man orders his life around godly counsel. Blessed is the man who walks not in the counsel of the ungodly. A man who follows the

Lord with his whole being does not want to seek advice from others just because they are successful.

A Godly man understands that he can still learn and that there is much he doesn't know.

A Godly man is not too proud to seek advice or too self-centered to ask for help.

A Godly man is always refreshed from the Word of God and his delight is in the law of the Lord.

A Godly person is fruitful. He invests his life in the lives of others. He does not live for a paycheck. Christ is more important than reaching the top of His profession. He is a faithful employee, but he loves bearing spiritual fruit. He is consistent. He doesn't wither under pressure.

He prospers in his home in his work in his finances and in his relationships. He will flourish in all that he does.

Let's look back at the life of Daniel. The angel Gabriel Daniel said he came in my extreme weariness. Gabriel addressed Daniel as one who was highly esteemed. One better than Gabriel has called you. Not only highly esteemed and of great value, but He gave His life to make you a Godly man.

Godly man character

(Character-is something to be sought after.)

Character is doing what is right because it is right. In Biblical terms, it's about righteous men who do what is right for the right reason. People of character don't make up the rules as they go along.

Men of character have not only agreed to God but morally they live it. They do what is right. Their personal obedience takes priority over personal achievement. Self-control is greater than self-fulfillment. It is all a matter of priorities.

Men who are quick to compromise their character do not know who they are. On the other hand, most of our problems as a nation stem from a lack of character among our leaders and citizens. Our biggest deficit in this nation is not a budget deficit, but a character deficit.

Return on Your Investments

Meeting your long-term investment goal is dependent on a number of factors. This includes your capital, your family, the way you live, where you spend your time and also the call that's on your life, your business and your ministry.

Men have been making investments all of their lives. The kingdom of God is the greatest investment in the world to invest in because it always take you back to your first love.

Revelation 2:4 (NKJ)

Yet I hold this against you: You have forsaken the love you had at first.

A Man Investment Questionnaire

1. Men, where are your investments?

2. What do you treasure in your life?

3. What does 'reap what you sow' mean?

4. Do you have your affairs in order?

5. Do you know where you are going to?

6. What do you value?

He gave us the ministry of reconciliation. His Love.

2 Corinthians 5:17(NIV)

Therefore from now on we regard no one according to the flesh. Even though we have known Christ according to the flesh, yet now we know Him thus no longer. Therefore if anyone is in Christ, he is a new creation. Old things have passed away, behold, all things have become new. Now all things are of God who has reconciled us to Himself through Jesus Christ, and has given us the ministry of reconciliation. That is that God was in Christ reconciling the world to Himself, not imputing their trespasses to them and has committed to us the word of reconciliation.

(It's time to embrace His love)

The Kingdom has an order and a system.

The order of Kingdom lifestyle is:

1. Pattern
2. Principals
3. Order

The Kingdom's system for man is:

1. God
2. Self
3. Marriage
4. Children
5. Work
6. Play

Value yourself because of God inside of you. It's okay to say, 'I am a man, but I act like God.' Don't look outside of yourself. Look in the mirror. The Word is the mirror.

James 1: 23-25(NKJ)

For if any be a hearer of the word and not a doer, he is like unto a man beholding his natural face in a glass. For he beholdeth himself, and goeth his way, and straightway forgetteth what manner of man he was. But whoso looketh into the perfect law of liberty, and continueth therein, he being not a forgetful hearer, but a doer of the work, this man shall be blessed in his deed.

Criminal minded men are always thinking they have a lawless soul. They think they can do what they want, when they want to do it. They have no respect for any kind of law or order in their life. The root is stubbornness and they will not hear correction. Most criminal minded men are:

1. Untouchable
2. Deceived
3. Self-Worship
4. Selfish
5. Very Controlling
6. Rage

I Samuel 15:23 (NKJ)

For rebellion is as the sin of witchcraft and stubbornness is as iniquity and idolatry.

A player or ladies man-a man who likes to have sexual relationships with more than one woman in his life.

Words related to:

1. Player
2. Pimp
3. Charmer
4. Playboy
5. Baller
6. Casanova

Lust of Flesh; Self-Centered Desire

This can have several contributing roots, but is always demonic-like. So many of the problems presented because of the lust of the world first having multiple sexual partners can result from curses. All sexual intercourse outside of marriage is fornication. Fornication as idolatry because fornication is considered idolatry and is a violation.

Colossians 3:5 (NKJ)

Therefore put to death your members which are on earth. Fornication, uncleanness, passion, evil desire and covetousness which is idolatry.

Deuteronomy 5:7 (NKJ)

Thou shalt have no other gods before me.

Rejection perceived by your parents especially the Father can be a root cause of multiple sexual partners.

Gay Men

I grew up around all kinds of people. My parents told me that God loved all people. And I believed that some of my old friends when I was in school were gay young men. I have family members who used to be gay but after they came back to Christ, they no longer lived that lifestyle.

Homosexual spirits can enter a person several ways. First it can be present while the child is still in the womb as a result of the sins of the father's. That's why men say 'I have always had this problem as long as I can remember.'

The curse of whoredom with the whoring spirit is described in Hosea 4:6-14, but the basic problem entrance of the perverse homosexual spirit is still idolatry from violation of God's law. Exodus 20:5 (NIV)

Romans 1:24-25 (NIV)

I believe what the Bible says about homosexuality because of idolatry. God gave them up to homosexual desire and activity. Wherefore God also gave them up to uncleanness through the lusts of their own hearts to dishonor their own bodies between themselves. Who changed the truth of God into a lie and worshipped and served the creature more than the Creator who is blessed forever. Amen.

A Man of God

Is a man who loves the Holy Spirit Jesus and God as one union a man who honors God with all of his spirit, substance and seed? A man who walks with God's glory on Him and he glorifies with his lips and his learning as well as his living? A man that is full with God's power, glory and honor=power. A man of God is a man whose will has been converted from self-will over to the will of thy Father.

A Spirit-formed man-is one who is living and walking in the image of God

He has shown you, O mortal, what is good and what does the Lord require of you to act justly and to love mercy and to walk humbly with your God.

1. Some men have children.
2. Some men don't have children.
3. Some men desire to be married.
4. Some men don't desire to be married.
5. Some men are religious.
6. Some men are spiritual.
7. Some men are evil.
8. Some men are tyrants.

9. Some men are leaders.
10. Some men are good.
11. Some men are lazy.
12. Some men are bold.
13. Some men are strong.
14. Some men are weak.
15. Some men are good fathers.
16. Some men are not good fathers.
17. Some men you can trust.
18. Some men you can't trust.
19. Some men have pride.
20. Some men are humble.

A Man with a Womb

From the place called kingdom, there is no male or female. God sees humanity and all humanity has a womb.

Womb-a place where something is generated, obsolete belly. An encompassing, protective, hollow or space.

Womb-is a carrier of the seed.

Seed-the term seed also has a general meaning that antedates anything that can be sown.

But this womb and seed is spiritual and every man has it but God can only start with a barren womb. First, let's look at some of the barren wombs in the Bible.

Barren-means unable to produce seed. Not fruitful.

Genesis 29:31 (NKJ)

And when the Lord saw that Leah was hated, he opened her womb, but Rachel was barren.

Judges 13:2-3 (NKJ)

A certain man of Zorah named Manoah from the clan of the Danites had a wife who was childless, unable to give birth. The angel of the Lord appeared to her and said, 'You are barren and childless, but you are going to become pregnant and give birth to a son. His name is Samson.'

You see, God is telling all men that it's a supernatural day in the kingdom of God and don't you let that day go by.

Then Manoah inquired of the angel of the Lord, 'What is your name so that we may honor you when your word comes true?' Judges 13:17 (NKJ)

The Spirit of God takes whole of the barren womb. It is the spirit that comes from the heart of God. It's called desire.

God is looking for a barren people. A people who cannot produce from out of their selves. The seed must be supernatural from God Himself. Jesus came from a supernatural seed and Mary's womb was barren. She was a virgin. When you are in the kingdom of God, you are now seed and He sees you as His remnant. All you need is faith of a mustard seed. Luke 17:6 (NKJ)

Anything more than a mustard seed is pride. Some men may never get married or they may never have children. We have a remnant of men that fits this category. The world looks at them as if something must be wrong with them, but it's not true. They are men who desire more than a wife and children. They are in a category of their own. And that does not mean they are gay. Most of them walk very close with God.

CHAPTER 7

IT'S TIME FOR THE BRIDE TO GO OVER

I received my salvation in 1993. I was a part of one ministry for about six years. Then the Holy Spirit came and released me and took me into the second ministry for about seven years and then He released me again.

Galatians 4:2 (NKJ)

You will be under tutors and governors until the time appointed of the Father.

Then, the Holy Spirit said to me, 'Go home and wait for me to come sit down at the table. Get your Bible and wait.' I sat for nine years reading and taking care of my own family.

1 John 2:27 (NKJ)

But the anointing which ye have received of him abideth in you and ye need not that any man teach you, but as the same anointing teacheth you all of things and is truth and is no lie and even as it hath taught you ye shall abide in Him.

It is time for his Bride's preparation and holy transformation for the work of the kingdom when we gave our life back we thought we were already in the kingdom. Now we have come out, it's time to go in. When you are connected to church organization you need to submit to the house vision and learn order because you have just come out of the world system.

But when you come into your day and hour, you must go all the way over into the kingdom of God. Then, the Holy Spirit will talk to you about your purpose.

Luke 12:12 (NKJ)

For the Holy Spirit will teach you in that very hour what you ought to do and say.

Jesus Is Our Pattern

Jesus did not come into His day and hour until the cross. Then His purpose was revealed. His purpose was to die. He came to the earth so He could be our pattern and to die.

The Kingdom of God is all about:

1. Patterns
2. Principle
3. Order

Death is separation. A physical death is the separation of the soul from the body. Spiritual death which is of greater significance is the separation of the soul from God in Genesis 2:17. God tells Adam that in the day he eats of the forbidden fruit, he will surely die. Adam does fall but his physical death does not occur immediately. God must have had another type of death in mind-spiritual death. This separation from God is exactly what we see in Genesis 3:8. When Adam and Eve heard the voice of the Lord, they hid themselves from the presence of the Lord God. The fellowship had been broken. They were spiritually dead.

When Jesus was hanging on the cross, He paid the price for us by dying on our behalf. Even though He is God, He is God. He still had to suffer the agony of a temporary separation from the Father due to the sin of the world He was carrying on the cross. After three hours of supernatural darkness, He cried, 'My God, my God, why hast thou forsaken me? Mark 15: 33-34 (NKJ)

This spiritual separation from the Father was the result of the Son taking our sins upon Himself. That the impact of sin. Sin is the exact opposite of God and God had to turn away from His own Son at that point in time. Anybody without Christ is spiritually dead.

The Bride is Christ's body, God is the Head and we are the Body. We must understand why the Bride must go over into the kingdom of God. There is no male or female in the kingdom so the Bride stands for men and women. Jesus is our Groom. We are always waiting for Him, never making a move without Him.

In December 2013 in Baltimore City, we had three days of summer-like weather in our city in these three days God shown me in the spirit where He released the flood of glory in our city but it came down out of the sky and laid down on the city very still. Then He told me to write letters to all of the chosen leaders in Baltimore's inner city and then He began to give me their names and faces. So I did what God asked me to do. He gave me Isaiah 40:31. (NKJ)

*Calling all the Eagles

This is the new beginning of apostolic power and authority in Baltimore City. Signs and wonders will accompany the called out ones. I am one of the head apostles of my generation. I know God is moving globally all over the world. But my assignment right now is Baltimore City.

The cloud and fire. We will always be safe if we obey the Lord. God has come to Baltimore City to clean up all of the religion and all of the witchcraft in most of the churches in our inner city the people are sating under a spell bound spirit.

You have boys and girls leading the people because of their gifts but they have no fruits in their lives that build the nature of God. They are ordaining each other and taking on title and roles God did not call them to . . But the day and hour is here for the mature sons of God to come forth, God's mature Bride, the true Church.

Now all of the sickness will be lifted up off the people, poverty, depression, hopelessness, oppression and mental illness. All of this comes from a false God-head called witchcraft. It's our time! Now your jig is up! The remnant is here and we will do it the way the Lord tells us to do it.

Isaiah 60:1 (NKJ)

Arise, shine for your light has come and the glory of the Lord rises upon you.

I keep talking about the hour because it's not the hour of the flesh, but the hour of the spirit.

The Bride is awakening to make herself ready by keeping the feasts until the two Christ and His Bride become one in soul as well as spirit in character and in works and in manifest splendor and glory throughout the earth. This book is not for religious Christians.

Stability-the state or quality of being stable.

Firmness in Position

Continuance without change; permanence.

Stability-is a word that goes with wisdom and God's knowledge. There were two men in the Bible that stood out to me who were unstable. Reuben was the first son of Jacob by his wife, Leah.

Genesis 49:4 (NKJ)

Unstable as water, you shall not have preeminence because you went up to your Father's bed then you defiled it, he went up to my couch.

The other person is Saul. Saul had many personalities. Saul looked like royalty. He was tall, handsome and noble. King Saul had the honor of being Israel's first king but his life turned into a tragedy for one reason. Saul did not trust in God. He became king when he was 30 years old and reigned over Israel 42 years. Early in his career, he made a fatal mistake. He disobeyed God by failing to completely destroy the Amalekites and all of their possessions as God had commanded. The Lord withdrew His favor from Saul and had Samuel the prophet anoint David as king. Because the people made more of David's single victory than all of Saul's. The king went into a rage and became jealous of David. From that moment, he plotted to kill him. King Saul needed stability in his time of reigning over Israel. Instead of building up Israel, King Saul wasted most of his time chasing David through the hills. David, however, respected God's anointed king and despite several opportunities, refused to harm Saul.

Scriptures for Stability

Psalms 40:2	Isaiah 40:8 (NKJ)
Proverbs 18:10	Isaiah 33:6
Jude 1: 24-25	Matthew 5:18
1 Peter 1:23-25	Matthew 24:35

Wisdom

If someone wanted to study the concept of wisdom in depth in the Bible, then starting with the book of Proverbs is recommended. Proverbs was mostly written by Solomon, the man to whom the Bible says God gave great wisdom.

Job 12:12 (NKJ)

And unto man he said, Behold, the fear of the Lord that is wisdom and to depart from evil is understanding.

Psalms 111:10(NKJ)

The fear of the Lord is the beginning of wisdom. A good understanding have all they that do his commandments. His praise endureth forever.

Proverbs 1:7 (NKJ)

The fear of the Lord is the beginning of knowledge but fools despise wisdom and instruction.

Wisdom (NKJ)

Proverbs 3:7   James 1:5

Proverbs 4:5-7   Ecclesiastes 7:12

Proverbs 9:10   Proverbs 11:30

The Bible says Psalm 1 that a person who meditates on God's Word will be blessed. The wisdom of the Bible will help guide a person to avoid wrong friends and influences. The wisdom of God will have life-giving nourishment that God provides through His Word.

Wisdom is the third dimension in God. It comes when you are in your seventh day, the Sabbath, the day of rest.

Hebrews 4:9-11 (NKJ)

There remaineth therefore a rest to the people of God. For he that is entered into his rest he also hat ceased from his own works as God did from his. Let us labor therefore to enter into that rest lest any man fall after the same example of unbelief.

What is the third dimension? A place in God. A royal place.

1. King Saul
2. King David
3. King Solomon

God chose Solomon to build his house. The house is His people.

Hosea 4:6-7 (NKJ)

My people are destroyed for lack of knowledge because you have rejected knowledge. I reject you from being a priest to me and since you have forgotten the law of your God, I also will forget your children. The more they increased, the more they sinned against me. I will change their glory into shame.

God is speaking to His people! Don't reject God's knowledge.

Proverbs 12:1 (NKJ)

Whoever loves discipline loves knowledge but he who hates reproofs is stupid.

1. Stay humble when God does start to release His knowledge to you.
2. Do not ever cease listening to instruction.
3. Knowledge and understanding wisdom comes direct from God.

CHAPTER 8

YOU NEED MORE THAN YOUR PASTOR

Why do we need more than our pastors? The word 'pastor' means 'a spiritual overseer; a clergyman serving a local church or parish or a shepherd.'

In Ephesians 4:11-12 (NKJ)

And He Himself gave some to be apostles, some prophets, some evangelists, and some pastors and teachers. For the equipping of the saints, for the work of ministry for the edifying of the body of Christ.

We need the five-fold ministry so the church can grow up into a mature body. And after the five gifts come into unity, it becomes a new priesthood called the Melchizedek priesthood. Melchizedek was one of those puzzling people in the Bible who appeared only briefly but are mentioned again as examples of holiness and right living. His name means 'king of righteousness' and his title 'King of Salem' also means 'king of peace.' The Bible does not shed any light on Melchizedek's religious rituals either except to mention that he brought out bread and wine for Abram. This act and Melchizedek's holiness have led some scholars to describe him as a type of Christ. One of those Bible people who show the same qualities as Jesus Christ, Savior of the World.

With no record of father or mother and no genealogical background in Scripture. This description is fitting. Other scholars go a step further theorizing that Melchizedek may have been a theophany of Christ or a manifestation of deity in temporary form.

Understanding Jesus's status as our high priest is a key point in the book of Hebrews. Just as Melchizedek was not born into the Levitical priesthood but was appointed by God, so Jesus was named our eternal high priest interceding with God the Father on our behalf.

Hebrews 5:8-10 (NKJ)

Though He was a son yet He learned obedience by the things which He suffered. And having been perfected, He became the author of eternal salvation to all who obey Him called by God as High Priest according to the order of Melchizedek.

This is what happens to people when they only have a pastor. Samuel warned the people nevertheless the people refused to obey the voice of Samuel and they said no but we will have a king over us that we also may be like all the nations and that our king may judge us and go out before us and fight our battles. And Samuel heard all the words of the people and he repeated them in the hearing of the Lord. So the Lord said to Samuel, Heed their voice and make them a king. I Samuel 8:19-22 (NKJ)

And they got their tall, handsome king. Saul was literally head and shoulders above everyone. They had every right to be proud. They had a king everyone could see. They didn't just have a king who bloomed from the heavens who was in a fiery pillar or swirling cloud or who somehow opened seas for them to go through. Here was a real king with skin from the time of Adam and Eve right on through today. We have not been content to have God as our ruler and to hear from God ourselves the five-fold gifts are to be a confirm word always second.

We must have that close relationship with God the Father, God the Son and God the Holy Spirit ourselves.

Old Wineskins

I received a phone call from two special people in my life. They wanted to see me and have fellowship with me so they came over to my house but before they came over, I asked God about the visit and He took me to verses in the Bible that talks about no one pours new wine into old wineskins. Mark 2:22

And no one pours new wine into old wineskins, otherwise the wine will burst the skins and both the wine and the wineskins will be ruined. No, they pour new wine into new wineskins. They came over and God gave me a word for them both. But Mark 2:22 was for me. (NKJ)

The word for my first guest I will call her the intercessor because that's what she do. The word comes from Hebrews 4:4 'rest'. The other person I will call her 'elder'. The word for this person comes from John 3:3. Jesus teaches Nicodemus about the new birth. I did what God told me to do but while we were fellowshipping, God moved in power and demonstration. I put the glass teapot on the stove. The teapot was still new so we could have tea. The water was boiling and then the pot burst water and glass went all over the stove. And then the smoke detector went off.

While I was cleaning up the glass and water, the Holy Spirit said very softly, 'You can't pour new wine into old wineskins.' Mark 2:22 (NKJ)

The Holy Spirit said, 'I know you love the people from the former days, but when I am pouring new wine in you, there must be a separating of yourself because this time you are hearing out of a higher level of consciousness in God. Former friends and family members don't understand that God is doing something new and different with you. And when God gets ready, He will bring it all back together according to His plans.

Luke 5:37-38 (NIV)

And no man putteth new wine into old bottles else the new wine will burst the bottles and be spilled and the bottles shall perish. But new wine must be put into new bottles and both are preserved.

Keys

1. Throw down our cherished old wineskins.
2. Take on a deeper vessel of fullness of purpose .

What is meant by 'old' wineskins? The phrase 'old wineskins' refers to yesterday's move of God. Yesterday's manna or last year's inspiration.

It's Time to Rest

Exodus 34:21 (NKJ)

Six days thou shalt work but on the seventh day, thou shalt rest in earing time and in harvest thou shalt rest.

Exodus 20:8-11(NKJ)

Remember the Sabbath day to keep it holy. Six days shalt thou labour and do all thy work, but the seventh day is the Sabbath of the Lord thy God; in it thou shalt not do any work. For in six days the Lord made heaven and earth the sea and all that's in them is and rested the seventh day. Wherefore the Lord blessed the Sabbath day and hallowed it.

Keeping the Sabbath or Shabbat is one of the ten marital pledges of Israel to her husband Jehovah. She was instructed to refrain form physical labor one day a week. Like Jehovah, (Genesis 2:2) she was to rest. Her obedience was originally tested and proven in the gathering of manna.

Mark 2:27 (NKJ)

The Sabbath was made for man and not man for the Sabbath.

For both Israel and the church the Sabbath is a gift; a wedding gift from the Groom to His beloved. It is intended to bless and benefit us. Jesus is Lord of the Sabbath and keeping it is evidence of our union with Him.

Hebrews 4:9-11 (NKJ)

There remaineth therefore a rest to the people of God. For he that is entered into his rest he also hath ceased from his own works, as God did from his. Let us labour therefore to enter into that rest, lest any man fall after the same example of unbelief. We must have a lifestyle of trust and faith in Christ our Lord in our day to day walk before an anxious fear-ridden world.

Having finished His work, He rested on the seventh day. There was nothing lacking. His work was complete at that point of perfection. God called human beings into His rest. The perfection that existed when God placed Adam and Eve in the garden is something that you and I cannot comprehend because we've never known anything but a fallen world. Once Adam and Eve made the choice to be disobedient and go their own way the option to enter God's rest was impossible.

Psalms 95:10-11 (NKJ)

For forty years, I was grieved with that generation and said, it is a people who go astray in their hearts and they do not know my ways so I swore in my wrath they shall not enter my rest.

It was never God's intention to enter the seventh day of rest alone. He created us to be His intimate companions and enjoy the finished work of creation in all its glory. He made it possible for us to enter the rest that had been waiting for us since creation. From the cross, Jesus said, 'It is finished,' but I wonder if anyone really understood what He was saying to those present that day and to us today.

The Father and the Son had their labor to perform. Nothing was lacking in God's creation and nothing is lacking in the completion of Jesus' resurrection from the grave. It's time to get out of our own head and stop always making a way for ourselves.

CHAPTER 9

THE REALM OF THE SOUL

Soul

Brain	Reason
Mind	Emotions and Feelings
Thought	
The deepest part of a human is their will.	

Converted

Human will ←--------------------------------------→ The Father's will

| |

Your Agenda   God's Agenda

Converted-change something's character; to change something from one character, form or function to another or be changed in character, form or function. The human will always question God's will.

Multiple Personalities

The double-minded person develops two or sometimes more personalities based on their reaction of either fear or pride rather than leaning on God for wisdom and following the Holy Spirit's leading. The personalities become more unstable. The degree of mental, spiritual instability depends on many factors including: REJECTION ITS FRUITS AND ITS ROOTS BY WILLIAM G. NULL, MD PAGE 253 COPYRIGHT 2005 PUBLISHED BY IMPACT CHRISTIAN BOOKS,INC

1. Family history and depth of past involvement in whoredom, idolatry and extreme legalism.
2. Amount of adverse pressure a person is receiving.
3. Length of time a person has been yielding to the spirits.

When the double-minded person is offended and under pressure, they react with those around them the results of their reactions are greatly influenced by the relative stability of those with whom they react. If the person with them they react is stable and has knowledge of their problem, then they can bind the fear and pride and its manifested fruit. Then they can with a spirit of gentleness correct them so that God might grant them repentance and a knowledge of the truth.

James 3:16 (KJV)

For where envy and self seeking exist, confusion and every evil thing are there.

Galatians 6:1 (KJV)

Brethren, if a man is overtaken in any trespass, you who are spiritual restore such a one in a spirit of gentleness, considering your self lest you also be tempted.

Heart

Heart-your spirit is in your heart.

Natural heart-the heart is a hollow, muscular organ that pumps blood throughout the blood vessels to various parts of the body by repeated rhythmic contractions.

Psalms 51:10 (NKJ)

Create in me a clean heart, O God, and renew a right spirit within.

Matthew 13:15 (NKJ)

For this people heart is waxed gross and their ears are dull of hearing and their eyes they have closed lest at anytime they should see with their eyes and hear with their ears and should understand with their heart, and should be converted and I should heal them.

Faith must first be from the heart.

Faith-cannot come from the soul because the soul has to be transformed.

Faith-cannot come from the flesh because the flesh has a smell to it.

If faith comes any other way, it will not last. It must come from the heart.

Heart

> Renew Spirit
> Heart to Heart
> Face to Face
> Spirit to Spirit

The Father's Will

God's Agenda

Write God's Word on the tablet of your heart.

Proverbs 7:3 (NKJ)

Bind them on your fingers; write them on the tablet of your heart.

This book of the law shall not depart out of thy mouth, but thou shalt meditate therein day and night that thou mayest observe to do according to all that is written therein. For then thou shalt make thy way prosperous and then thou shalt have good success. Joshua 1:8 (NKJ)

Deuteronomy 6:5-12 (NKJ)

And thou shalt love the Lord thy God with all thine heart and with all thy soul and with all thy might. And these words which I command thee this day shall be in thine heart. And thou shalt teach them diligently unto thy children and shalt talk of them when thou sittest in thine house and when thou walkest by the way and when thou liest down and when thou risest up. And thou shalt bind them for sign upon thine hand and they shall be as frontlets between thine eyes. And thou shalt write them upon the posts of thy house and on thy gates.

And it shall be when the Lord thy God shall have brought thee in to the land which he swore unto thy fathers to Abraham, to Isaac and to Jacob to give thee great and goodly cities which thou buildest not. And houses full of good things which thou filledst not and wells digged which thou diggest not. Vineyards and olive trees which thou plantedst not when thou shalt have eaten and be full. Then beware lest thou forget the Lord which brought thee forth out of the land of Egypt from the house of bondage.

Obscurity of the Soul

Obscurity-dim, dark increasing darkness, to hide darken heavy fog, not clear, hard to understand, to make less clear, remote out of the way, unknown, lack of clear meaning.

Darkness of the Soul

Isaiah 29:18 (NKJ)

Isaiah 58:10 (NKJ)

Isaiah 59:9 (NKJ)

The soul-earthquakes

The heavens-trembles

Double-Minded Reaction-comes from reaction out of the soulish realm. The two-fold double-minded reactions of the flesh to rejection are fear and pride.

Ezekiel 16:3 (NKJ)

Thus says the Lord God to Jerusalem, Your birth and your nativity are from the land of Canaan. Your father was an Amorite-(pride) and your mother a Hittite-(fear).

Fear

Since rejection is a denial of love, the first reaction is to turn inward to the safety of fantasy where you are in control. There you can find love and acceptance in the privacy and safety of your mind. In the process, you become God, controlling events to your desired outcome.

Fear is acted out of your soulish realm.

Fantasy is acted out of your soulish realm.

Words that are connected to Fear

Insecurity and Inferiority-the grasshopper spirit manifests with withdrawal, isolation and constant fear of failure, self-hate and a desire to return to bondage.

Torment-manifests through recurrent panic attacks and nightmares consistent fear of dark fear of germs and harassing thoughts and mental confusion.

Self-Pity-is manifested by a feeling of unfairness with envy and jealousy which sometimes manifest as anger and rage. Also false compassion and false responsibility.

Terror-is manifested as occasional panic attacks, but usually as depression. The depression is either somnolent depression, tired and sleepy or reactive depression with hyperactivity acting out flight of ideas, extremely talkative and mood swings passive-aggressive. This often results in drug use and sometimes suicide.

Perfectionism-is when the person takes refuge behind the rulebook Mosaic Law, denominational creed, employee handbook and civil services rules. If you do everything perfectly according to the rulebook, you are secure. This opens you to all of the problems of perfectionism, fear of mistakes, rechecking work(yours and others), constructive criticism, pride, ego, critical spirit, impatience, anger, rage and violence. Book Rejection by William G.Null M.D Page45.

Paranoia-is accompanied by feelings of envy and jealousy, distrust and imagined persecution. There is also deception so that the person cannot see the truth.

As all of these problems manifest in your life, they cause other people to avoid and reject you.

Pride

Pride-haughty, arrogant, stubborn, unteachable, rebellious and unable to receive correction, these traits are basic, outward reactions from the soul.

Proverbs 21:24(KJV)

A proud and haughty man, Scoffer is his name, he acts with arrogant pride.

Proverbs 15:12 (KJV)

A scorner loveth not one that reproveth him; neither will he go unto the wise.

Proverbs 22:10(KJV)

Cast out the scorner and contention shall go out, yea strife and reproach shall cease.

Ten Ways to Nourish the Soul

1. Meditate-is a practice in which an individual trains the mind or induces a mode of consciousness either to realize some benefit or as an end in itself.
2. Integrate-a pure awareness of your soul. Make something open to all, to make a group, community place or organization and its opportunities.
3. Fall in Love-make every part of life the joy and the sorrow, the losses and the gains part of the spiritual search.
4. Spiritual Memory-pictures, letters, music, garden also seeing the beloved in other people, your nose smelling always for the scent of God.
5. Take Care of Yourself-physical, mental and emotional health and well-being nourish the soul.
6. Create Ritual-as long as the rituals are fresh and new, take time alone with friends and family to give honor and celebrate life.
7. Slow Down-too much speed kills the appreciation of the soul. If your life is crammed with activity, get rid of some of it, make downtime a priority.
8. Love Other People-the most powerful way to open up to the truth of the soul is to love other people, animals, nature and life itself.
9. Remove the Barriers-don't force the soul to reveal itself. It can't be done. Soul is already here. Our work is to get out of the way.
10. Lean Back into God's Perfect Plan-the more we identify with the soul, the more spacious and willing we become in our approach

to life. When everything is experienced as part of our eternal soul's journey, we can relax. We can let go into the plan of God.

Duality and Unity

The two has become one, the soul and the spirit. The soul by itself has a conflicting pull. The soul is like a wave approaching the ocean shore. I can feel God pulling me toward his oneness just as the sea calls to the wave. I have a desire to live as a wave as an individual soul a single personality. I existed in a vibrant and peaceful relationship between form and formless between the born and the unborn between my soul and God.

Spiritual practice is remembering over and over that we are involved in this life and that peace and happiness resides in our ability to transcend duality even as we live within it.

This is the fulfillment of the spiritual quest the release from the painful struggle of duality. As long as our consciousness is trapped on the dualistic plane. Our soul feels cramped to release our souls from this cramped existence to cease the struggle of duality and to awaken in to the freedom of unity. You and God.

The soul and spirit became one like a marriage. The soul must submit so the pull can stop between the two. I learned this life lesson during the time when I lay to rest my 24 year old son. Because some conceive of death as the opposite of life; life on the dualistic plane feels like a continuous problem. Because we don't experience how life and death are just two sides of the same coin. We cling to life and fear death. And out of this basic misconception of reality, all other misconceptions are born. In duality consciousness, we live in a world of struggle, a world of opposites. We can live with a passionate devotion to our differences and at the same time take our place in this world with others and all of life. Then we will have found unity within duality because I have found the giver of joy-God.

When we discover the Giver of Joy, we will find unity within ourselves. We will stop fearing the opposite of happiness or the opposite of success or the opposite of love.

Unity-it cleanses the soul.

Opposites become partners.

New International Version

Even the darkness will not be dark to you; the night will shine like the day for darkness is as light to you.

International Standard Version

Even darkness isn't dark to you; darkness and light are the same to you.

Scriptures

1 John 1:5	John 12:25
Matthew 18:21	Acts 20:35
John 20:29	Isaiah 45:7
Amos 3:6	

The Twelve Gates were Twelve Pearls

The soul must come through the twelve gates. We need healing; we need deliverance. That comes before we experience freedom.

The Twelve Tribes of Israel

Jacob's new name is 'Israel' which means 'ruling with God.' Israel had twelve sons whose descendants became the twelve tribes. The tribes were collectively known as the nation Israel.

Each tribe is a pearl.

Each tribe is a gate.

Each is an experience and an expression of his nature.

1. There is a gate of grace. It's the high praise of deliverance called the pearl of Judah.
2. There is a gate of grace we go through called a troop. It is where we experience the battle and find total victory. It is the pearl of Gad.
3. There is a gate of grace we go through called happiness. It is the pearl of Asher.
4. There is a gate of grace we go through that causes us to forget our past hurts and trauma called the pearl of Manassah.
5. There is a gate of grace called hearing. This is when our ears are opened to revelation knowledge. It is the pearl of Simeon.
6. There is a gate of grace we must go through called a habitation of rest. It is called the pearl of Zebulon.
7. There is a gate of grace we go through that joins us together as one. It is called the pearl of Levi.

8. There is a gate of grace we go through called divine increase. It is the pearl of Ephraim.

9. There is a gate of grace we go through where our focus changes from being a servant to behold a son. It is called the pearl of Reuben. Unstable as water.

10. There is a gate of grace we go through; the son of my right hand speaks of authority and favor. It is called the pearl of Benjamin.

11. There is a gate of grace we go through where we find our reward. It is not in earthly success or perishable things but in Christ. It is called the pearl of Issachar.

12. There is a gate of grace we go through where we know what it is to be left alone and wrestle unto a new day. It is the pearl of Naphtali.

Each gate of the city is an experience we have in Christ that produced a pearl. Something that will not be taken away. The experience becomes a precious pearl.

Revelation 21:27 (NKJ)

The twelve gates were twelve pearls each individual gate was one pearl. And the street of the city was pure gold like transparent glass.

<u>The Glory of the New Jerusalem</u>

But I saw no temple in it for the Lord God Almighty and the Lamb are its temple. The city had no need of the sun or the moon to shine in it for the glory of God illuminated it. The Lamb is its light. And the nations of those who are saved shall walk in its light and the kings of the earth bring their glory and honor into it.

Its gates shall not be shut at all by day. There shall be no night there. And they shall bring the glory and the honor of the nations into it.

But there shall by no means enter it. Anything that defiles or causes an abomination or a lie, but only those who are written in the Lamb's Book of Life.

Making Everything New

Now I saw a new heaven and a new earth, for the first heaven and the first earth had passed away. Also there was no more sea.

Then I John saw the holy city New Jerusalem coming down out of heaven from God prepared as a bride adorned for her husband. And I heard a loud voice from heaven saying, Behold, the tabernacle of God is with men and He will dwell with them and they shall be His people. God Himself will be with them and be their God. Revelation 21:1-3 (NKJ)

To understand the mystery of the kingdom, we must have spiritual understanding because the author of this book is spirit. Let's look at the city and see what the Father is talking about:

The city is a people. The 'abode' means home for the fullness of God=body of Christ=the Bride=Lamb's wife=the church in glory and perfection. (NKJ)

John 14:2-23   1 Cor. 3:9-16
Ephesians 2:19-22   2 Cor. 5:1
Rev. 3:12 2   Timothy 2:20

Mansion-Greek word 'mone' (NKJ)

John 14:2
John 14:23

Whose mansion? Father's house, not yours.

Word made Flesh=Dwelt=Tabernacle=House John 1:14 (NKJ)

In the purest sense, Jesus was a house, an 'abode', a habitation for the fullness of God.

Mone-primarily a staying; an abiding to abide. This mansion, this abode, this dwelling place, is it for me? Or is it for Him? I Chronicles 29:1 (NKJ)

The abode (home) of God is with men. Revelation 21:3 (NKJ)

Jesus Himself called us a city full of light. Matthew 5:13-14(NKJ)

The Twelve Gates
Twelve Pearls
Twelve Experiences
Twelve Angels
Twelve Messengers
Twelve Messages
Twelve Fruits

The number 12 is God's government. He is unfolding the divine nature from (within you. (NKJ)

Colossians 1:26-29   Revelations 22:1-5
2 Peter 1:1-4   Genesis 49:1
Galatians 4:19   Revelations 21:12-13

Each of the twelve gates is a manifestation of the nature of God in you kicking hard to be birthed from within. Each is an experience and an expression of His nature.

CONCLUSION

Invasion of God's glory in Baltimore City will shut down all of the hospitals because they will be at an all-time low of sick people in the city. The hospital system will lose millions of dollars. Crime and violence will also be at an all-time low.

This glory will be awakening this city God has called the remnant to come together on one accord in the spirit realm.

Remnant-small part still left. A small part of something that remains after the rest has gone to sleep.

Realm-kingdom, a county ruled by a nation of people.

The Invasion of God's glory is the Day of Pentecost, it's Harvest Time for Baltimore City, it's a Supernatural Day. Hear the word for Baltimore City.

Jeremiah 23 (NKJ)
(The Lord and His sheep)

Woe to the shepherds who destroy and scatter the sheep of my pasture. This is the Lord's declaration therefore this is what the Lord the God of Israel says about the shepherds who shepherd my people. You have scattered my flock, banished them and have not attended to them. I will attend to you because of your evil acts the Lord, declaration. I will gather the remnant of my flock from all the lands where I have banished them and I will return them to their grazing land. They will become fruitful and numerous. I will raise up shepherds over them who will shepherd them. They will no longer be afraid or dismayed, nor will any be missing. This is the Lord's declaration.

(The Righteous Branch of David)

The days are coming; this is the Lord's declaration when I will raise up a righteous Branch of David. He will reign wisely as king and administer justice and righteousness in the land. In His day, Judah will be saved and Israel will dwell securely. This is what He will be named, 'The Lord is our Righteousness.' The days are coming the Lord's declaration when it will no longer be said as the Lord lives who brought the Israelites from the land of Egypt but as the Lord lives who brought and led the descendants of the house of Israel from the land of the north and from all of the other countries where I had banished them. They will dwell once more in their own land.

(False Prophets Condemned)

Concerning the prophets
My heart is broken within me
And all my bones tremble
I have become like a drunkard
Like a man overcome by wine
Because of the Lord
Because of His Holy Words
For the land is full of adulterers
The land mourns because of the curse
And the grazing lands in the wilderness have dried up.

Their way of life has become evil and their power is not rightly used because both prophets and priests are ungodly. Even in my house I have found their evil. This is the Lord's declaration. Therefore their way will be to them like slippery paths in the gloom. They will be driven away and fall down there. For I will bring disaster on them the year of their punishment. This is the Lord's declaration. Among the prophets of Samaria, I saw something disgusting. They prophesied by Baal and led my people Israel astray. Among the prophets of Jerusalem also I saw a horrible thing. They commit adultery and walk in lies. They strengthen the hands of evildoers and none turns his back on evil. They are all like Sodom to me. Jerusalem's residents are like Gomorrah.

Therefore this what the Lord of Hosts says concerning the prophets. I am about to feed them wormwood and give them poisoned water to drink for from the prophets of Jerusalem ungodliness has spread throughout the land. This is what the Lord of Hosts says. Do not listen to the words of the prophets who prophesy to you. They are making you worthless. They speak visions from their own minds not from the Lord's mouth. They keep on saying to those who despise me. The Lord has said you will have peace. To everyone who walks in the stubbornness of his hearts they have said, no harm will come to you.

For who has stood in the council of the Lord to see and hear His Word? Who has paid attention to His Word and obeyed? Look, a storm from the Lord. Wrath has gone forth. A whirling storm. It will whirl about the head of the wicked.

The Lord's anger will not turn back until He has completely fulfilled the purposes of His heart. In time to come, you will understand it clearly. I did not send these prophets yet they ran with a message. I did not speak to them yet they prophesied. If they had really stood in my council, they would have enabled my people to hear my words and would have turned them back from their evil ways and their evil deeds. Am I a God who is only near this is the Lord's declaration and not a God who is far away? Can a man hide himself in secret places where I cannot see him? The Lord's declaration. Do I not fill the heavens and the earth? The Lord's declaration. I have heard what the prophets who prophesy a lie in my name have said, 'I had a dream, I had a dream.' How long will this continue in the minds of the prophets prophesying lies, prophets of the deceit of their own minds?

Through their dreams that they tell one another, they make plans to cause my people to forget my name as their fathers forgot my name through Baal worship. The prophet who has only a dream should recount the dream but the one who has my word should speak my word truthfully for what is straw compared to grain (the Lord's declaration). Is not my word like fire (the Lord's declaration) and like a sledgehammer that pulverizes rock? Therefore take note; I am against the prophets (the Lord's declaration) who steal my words from each other.

I am against the prophets (the Lord's declaration) who use their own tongues to deliver an oracle. I am against those who prophesy false dreams (the Lord's declaration) telling them and leading my people astray with their falsehoods and their boasting. It was not I who sent or commanded them and they are of no benefit at all to these people. This is the Lord's declaration.

Restoration for the City of Baltimore City

Psalm 85:1-13 (NKJ)

You showed favor to your land, O Lord, you restored the fortunes of Jacob. You forgave the iniquity of our people and covered all their sins. You set aside all your wrath and turned from your fierce anger. Restore us again, O God, our Savior and put away your displeasure toward us. Will you be angry with us forever? Will you prolong your anger through all generations? Will you not revive us again that your people may rejoice in you? Show us your unfailing love, O Lord and grant us your salvation. I will listen to what God the Lord will say. He promises peace to his people his saints but let them not return to folly. Surely his salvation is near those who fear him that his glory may dwell in our land. Love and faithfulness meet together. Righteousness and peace kiss each other. Faithfulness springs forth from the earth and righteousness looks down from heaven. The Lord will indeed give what is good and our land will yield its harvest. Righteousness goes before him and prepares the way for his steps.

Harvest Time

REFERENCES

1. Strong's Exhaustive Concordance of the Bible by James Strong. Copyright 1975-1976
2. Life Application Bible, New King James Version by Tyndale House
3. The Passion Bible by Holman, Christian Standard Bible Copyright 2004
4. Rejection by William G. Null MD. Copyright 2005